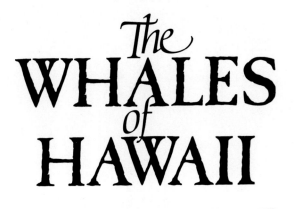

The WHALES of HAWAII

Cuvier's beaked whale [Heinrich Schatz]

Bottlenose dolphins (Gerard M. Wellington)

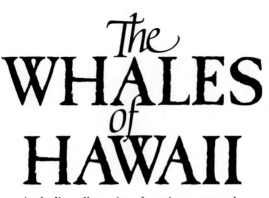

The WHALES of HAWAII

*including all species of marine mammals
in Hawaiian and adjacent waters*

produced by
**STANLEY M.
MINASIAN**

written by
**KENNETH C.
BALCOMB III**

illustrated by
**LARRY
FOSTER**

A PUBLICATION OF THE MARINE MAMMAL FUND

Library of Congress Cataloging-in-Publication Data

Balcomb, Kenneth C., 1940-
   The whales of Hawaii, including all species of marine
mammals in Hawaiian and adjacent waters.

   1. Cetacea—Hawaii.   2. Hawaiian monk seal.
3. Marine mammals—Hawaii. 4. Mammals—Hawaii.
I. Minasian, Stanley M., 1947-   . II. Foster,
Larry, 1934-   . III. Marine Mammal Fund. IV. Title.
QL737.C4B236   1987   599.5'09969   86-33149
ISBN 0-961■7803-0-4 (pbk.)

Printed in Hong Kong by Ad Color

Copy Editing: Jake Widman
Book Design and Production: Dustin Kahn
Cover Photo: James D. Watt,
Humpback Whale and Calf

STANLEY M. MINASIAN began the Marine Mammal Fund in 1971 as a nonprofit organization devoted to public education and research on marine mammals and ocean issues. Through the Fund, he has produced and directed two nationally televised documentary films, one on the status of the great whales and a second, which won three Emmy Awards on the incidental killing of dolphins during commerical tuna fishing operations. He is currently producing and directing a documentary film on the endangered Hawaiian monk seal. Stan, with Kenneth C. Balcomb III, co-authored *The World's Whales*, a definitive guide to whales, dolphins, and porpoises published by Smithsonian Books in 1984. He was born and resides in San Francisco, California.

KENNETH C. BALCOMB III was raised in the flatlands of New Mexico and central California before attending the University of California and graduating with a Bachelor of Arts degree in Zoology in 1963. He worked as a whale biologist for the United States Fish and Wildlife Service and as a field biologist for the United States National Museum before joining the navy to become an aviator and oceanographer. From 1976 to 1986, Ken was chief scientist for the Ocean Research and Education Society (ORES) in Massachusetts. In this capacity he designed the whale research and student education programs for the research barquentine *Regina Maris*, and he was the onboard scientist for most of her expeditions in the Atlantic and eastern central Pacific oceans. He now resides in Friday Harbor, Washington, where he is Director of Research for two oceanographic ships operated by Intersea Research, Inc. for participant studies of whales in Alaska, Hawaii, and the South Pacific. He dedicates this book to his mother, Barbara Bales, who lives in Honolulu.

LARRY FOSTER was born in Sacramento, California, and cannot remember a time when he was not interested in whales. He is probably the world's leading authority on the shapes and sizes of whales, dolphins, and porpoises. Dr. James Mead, Curator of Marine Mammals at the Smithsonian Institution, has said, ''Larry has turned whale illustration into a science. His illustrations are the most anatomically accurate I have ever seen.'' Larry's work has appeared in many books and magazines, including *The World's Whales*, published by Smithsonian Books, and *National Geographic*.

TABLE OF CONTENTS

Striped dolphins (Robert L. Pitman)

Hawaiian monk seal (Stanley M. Minasian)

PREFACE

The Whales of Hawaii was written to introduce visitors and residents alike to the marine mammals of this magnificent island system. While humpback whales, which migrate to Hawaii each winter for mating and birthing, are Hawaii's best-known marine mammals, over twenty species swim in Hawaiian waters at some time during the year, including one species of seal found nowhere else in the world. There may well be even more species than those listed in this book, for the study of these enigmatic creatures is relatively young and some may still be unknown to us.

The pages of this book are filled with the finest photographs available, although not all were taken in Hawaiian waters. Where photographs of particular species were not available, carefully researched illustrations were included instead.

This publication is brought to you by the Marine Mammal Fund, a nonprofit organization dedicated to the preservation of marine mammals and their environment through public education programs. Your enjoyment of this book will greatly contribute to the fulfillment of that goal.

We wish to thank the following persons and organizations who greatly assisted in making this book a reality: John Dougherty and all our friends at McDougall Press, William Gilmartin, Sea Life Park, Edward Shallenberger, Colin Willock of Survival Anglia Limited, Birgit Winning, Marineland of Florida, Ken Minasian, Lou Silva, Stephen Leatherwood, Dustin Kahn, Jake Widman, and countless others.

Stanley M. Minasian
President
Marine Mammal Fund

False killer whales with rough-toothed dolphin (Robert L. Pitman)

INTRODUCTION

Hawaii is surrounded by marine animals of many species that lend a very special character to this island paradise. The word "paradise" conjures up thoughts of lush vegetation and warm climate; but paradise does not end at the base of the precipitous cliffs and the volanoes we see meet the shore around us. It continues downward through beautiful and diverse fringing reefs and outward to the clear blue waters of the vast Pacific Ocean. Most of the animal life which occurs in the geographically young archipelago of Hawaii is marine, including all of the oldest inhabitants of the region.

The most highly evolved of these ancient marine animals are the mammals—whales, dolphins, and seals—warm-blooded creatures of the sea which preceded other mammals and people to the archipelago by tens of millions of years. Their ancestors no doubt arrived before the islands erupted from the floor of the Pacific Ocean. Some came to the region for food, and some came for breeding and resting. Some evolved a lifestyle that keeps them here year-round, while others used the area as a "stopping point" in migration. Some visited with certain oceanic conditions. Some visited with the seasons. Others simply strayed into the area from faraway seas. These various patterns of distribution prevail today.

In total, the marine mammal species which occur around Hawaii comprise a fauna that is among the most spectacular of any in the world; but because these creatures inhabit the water, they go largely unseen except by those who learn of them and their ways.

This book is designed to acquaint the reader with the broad spectrum of marine mammals which typically occur around the Hawaiian Islands and to provide a glimpse of their wondrous lives. Most people will never see any of these animals in the wild because their habitat is so foreign and often remote to us. Some people will see a few of the larger and more spectacular species because they took care to look in the right places at the right times. Nobody will see all of them, nor is it even possible to list them all, because as a group they are still mysterious to us, and some may still be unknown. It is this sense of mystery that attracts us to their study. Yet for every fact we learn and appreciate, dozens remain unknown. Fortunately, an increasing number of researchers and naturalists are working to unravel the mysteries of these animals' lives and status as humanity increasingly exploits and alters their watery home. Hopefully, with that knowledge and with human interest and awareness of their habitat needs, we can enjoy the marine mammals of Hawaii and ensure their survival for future generations.

You, the reader, are part of that interest and awareness from the moment you pick up this book, or experience the exhilaration of seeing a herd of dolphins frolic around the bow of your boat, or witness a forty-ton whale leap into the air performing a graceful pirouette before landing with a tremendous splash. Keep up that excitement, but remember there are rules for the benefit of all.

Federal regulations in the form of the Marine Mammals Protection Act of 1972, make it a violation of the law to harass whales or any other marine mammal while they are in U.S. waters. Particular regulations apply concerning humpback whales in their breeding and calving areas around Hawaii: do not approach within one hundreds yards of them. No one has read the rules to the whales yet, so they may still approach you. The point is to let the whales establish what they want to do.

Even outside the hundred-yard limit, it is illegal to behave in a manner which is bothersome to whales (such as speeding in circles around them, or flying over them at low altitude). The rules are meant to prevent these whales from moving to other breeding grounds or from becoming extinct. One final word of advice for those out on a whale watching boat: look under the boat occasionally, as a whale could be closer than you think.

Humpback whale (Kenneth J. Minasian)

FIN WHALE
Balaenoptera physalus

Fin whales, while uncommon in tropical waters, may come within 200 miles of Hawaii during winter months, when they disperse throughout the lowest latitudes of their distribution. The breeding and calving season of the North Pacific stock of fin whales extends from about November to March (with the peak in December), during which time the breeding animals may be found in small groups in subtropical latitudes, with some groups venturing to the south of the main islands of Hawaii. (Unlike humpback whales, fin whales do not seem to congregate in specific, geographically identifiable breeding areas.) Some may even find suitable food supplies in the lower latitudes and remain after the breeding season. One group of eight to twelve enormous fin whales was observed by the author on 20 May 1966, about 250 miles south of Honolulu. They were associated with many thousands of sooty/slenderbill shearwaters and hundreds of dolphins in a tremendous feeding aggregation. There has also been a sighting near Hawaii, and one stranding reported in the islands.

Fin whales are the second largest animals on earth, reaching lengths of over 70 feet and weights greater than 100 tons. In contrast to their enormous size, they are sleek and streamlined, with a prominent dorsal fin that appears a second or so after the misty columnar "blow" of exhalation. These are clues to identification at a distance; at close range, identification is confirmed by the asymmetrical coloration of the head, which is lighter on the right side with a pure white lower right lip and throat. The left of the head and throat, as well as the back and sides, is gun-metal grey except for a lighter-colored chevron pointing forward over the flippers. Often the coloration will be masked slightly by a green or brown patchy haze, caused by a film of diatoms adhering to the skin.

6

Fin whale calves are born looking just like adults. They are weaned at between six and eight months of age. (Painting by Larry Foster)

Sexual maturity occurs at age 8 to 12 when males are about 58 feet and females 60 feet in length. The gestation period is 11 to 12 months. Newborn fin whale calves are about 20 feet in length and weigh two or more tons; they nurse for about six months, by which time they weigh about 10 tons. Their lifespan ranges normally from 50 to 80 years; and, there does not appear to be a decrease in fertility with age. Females may bear a dozen young in their lifetime.

Fin whales usually travel in herds of half a dozen to a hundred or more, but the distance between animals in the herd may at times be measured in miles. As noted whale researcher Roger Payne once put it, "herd" might well be "heard" in the case of the huge baleen whales, whose contact with one another is largely acoustic: all whales of their kind within hearing range of 20 to 30 miles could be said to comprise the herd. Certainly, groups and individuals of this species coordinate their large-scale movements, coming and going according to patterns we only crudely recognize. The North

Pacific fin whales travel north for the summer and south for the winter; little else is known. Virtually nothing is known about the relationship among traveling companions. We literally know more about the solar system than we know about the social dynamics of whales.

Fin whales are very social animals, sometimes traveling in herds of a dozen to one hundred or more, diving and swimming in unison. (Kenneth C. Balcomb III)

BRYDE'S WHALE
Balaenoptera edeni

Bryde's (pronounced "Broodas") whales are unique among filter-feeding whales in spending their entire lives in tropical and subtropical waters. Throughout the world, their distribution is concentrated in waters whose temperature is between 65 and 80 degrees Fahrenheit, or roughly the waters between the equator and about 35 degrees latitude. Virtually all of the larger rorquals (the family of whales to which blue, Bryde's, fin, sei, humpback, and minke whales belong) range to temperate and polar regions for much of their feeding season, because polar waters are generally much more productive of the plankton upon which they feast. The tropics, while vast, generally lack suitable prey for filter-feeders. Nonetheless, Bryde's whales harvest the swarms which do occur and they are not as choosy about their diet as their larger relatives. Several species of euphausids, plus copepods, anchovies, sardines, herring, and jack mackerel have been found in the stomachs of Bryde's whales from various parts of the world.

The nearest that whaling for this species ever came to Hawaii was the operation of Japanese and Soviet whaling fleets west of the Leeward Islands in the early 1970s, when rather few whales were taken. This species has been hunted most extensively around the western rim of the Pacific, with catches of generally a few hundred *per annum*. The Central Pacific population of Bryde's whales has been conservatively estimated at 8,000 to 9,000 animals, and it is virtually unexploited except along the western rim.

In the region where they have been studied, there are two forms of Bryde's whales, one inshore and one offshore. The two feed and are distributed differently, and they even have different physical features. Those around Hawaii are most likely a part of the offshore form, which is the larger of the two. Their maximum size is about

9

Confirmed sightings of Bryde's whales are rare in Hawaiian waters, although their range extends throughout tropical and warm temperate waters around the world. (Richard Sears/MICS)

45 feet, although the average is 39 to 42 feet, with females slightly larger than males. Body weight is about 15 tons for adults.

Sexual maturity occurs between 8 and 11 years of age, and maximum life span is around 55 years, although the normal life span is in the forties. The length at sexual maturity is around 39 to 40 feet, females already being larger than males. The breeding season extends over much of the year, and the calving interval is approximately two years. Gestation is 12 months; the calf is born at about 14 feet in length; and weaning occurs after six months, when the calf has grown to about 25 feet in length.

In overall appearance, Bryde's whales have a streamlined torpedo shape. The rostrum (head) is V-shaped, but slightly rounded toward the front, and there is a median ridge which extends along the top from the tip of the rostrum to the blowhole. Two smaller ridges run parallel to the median ridge, one on each side, a feature unique to this species. Unless the ridges are visible (see accompanying photograph), one cannot definitely distinguish a Bryde's whale from a large minke or a sei whale. In fact, for most of whaling history, Bryde's whales have been misidentified as sei whales, even on the flensing deck by professional whalers and whale biologists. The dorsal fin is large (up to 18 inches tall), curved to the rear, and often scarred or ragged along its back edge. The body coloration is gun-metal grey on the top and lighter underneath, with grey overall pockmarks inflicted by bites from small cookie-cutter sharks. (These aggressive little pelagic sharks take ice cream scoop-size bites out of the hides of many marine mammal species in the tropics; the scars from their bite were known long before the sharks themselves were discovered.) Bryde's whales are typically observed singly, one every few square miles in the areas where they are numerous. They are not known to form herds, and observations at sea indicate that their swimming behavior is evasive and erratic, with frequent changes of course while underwater. Bryde's whales are rarely seen around Hawaii, though these waters are certainly within their range.

Bryde's whales are readily identified by the smaller secondary ridges on the top of the head, one on each side of the central ridge. (Bernie Tershy and Craig Strong)

MINKE WHALE
Balaenoptera acutorostrata

Minke whales are uncommon in Hawaiian waters, though they are quite numerous in some part of the world. The reason for their scarcity in the tropics might be that without a thick layer of blubber to last them for long migrations and periods without eating, they have to stay relatively near planktonic food supplies and in higher latitudes. Hawaii's beautiful clear, blue, warm waters simply support little of the plankton life upon which filter feeders depend. The occasional minke whale does pass through this region, but the chances of seeing one are slim.*

There is a distinct tendency for minke whales to segregate by sex and age, at least for portions of the year. The oldest and largest whales tend toward higher latitudes and highly productive waters, while the younger and smaller whales tend toward less extreme latitudes and less productive waters. Both the northern and southern populations shift toward the poles in the summer and toward the equator in the winter, but in rather indistinct migrations. From this, we might expect any minke whales around the Hawaiian archipelago to be smaller and younger than those further north, and they are more likely to be seen in winter months.

In the North Pacific Ocean, minke whales grow to about 27 feet in length and 7 tons, with the female being slightly larger than the male. The body coloration is slate black on top with swaths of lighter grey sweeping up from the thorax, meeting in a chevron pattern on the back just ahead of the dorsal fin. The belly is creamy grey to white, and there is a distinct wide band of white across the flipper, which is characteristic of this species in the Northern

*The author has seen only one near the Hawaiian Islands, that being a juvenile that rode the bow wave of a navy ship for about two hours just south of Honolulu.

12

In this extremely rare underwater photograph, the characteristic white patch on the flippers of minke whales is clearly evident. Note the pointed head, large flukes, and well-developed dorsal fin. (Howard Suzuki)

Hemisphere. (Some Southern Hemisphere minke whales lack this "armband".) The rostrum is sharply pointed, V-shaped as viewed from above, and it has a distinct ridge running from the tip of the snout to the blowholes on top of the head. The blow is faint, rising in a vertical bushy column to a height of about 6 feet, and it is difficult to see in tropical atmosphere. The dorsal fin stands a foot or slightly more in height, and is sharply pointed and sickle-shaped. The flukes are virtually never raised above the water. Minke whales breach or leap from the water only rarely but may do so when excited or alarmed, and they may porpoise through the water, making low-angle leaps from the surface to breathe.

The natural history of minke whales is fairly well known, due to extensive hunting of this species in recent years following the demise of larger whales. Sexual maturity is reached at age 6 or 7 at a length of 20 to 23 feet (males and females respectively), and the natural lifespan is about 50 years. The breeding and calving season extends from late spring to late fall, and the calving interval is two years. Gestation takes about one year, and young are weaned within six months. Food species include herring, euphausids, and copepods.

Minke whales are protected in U.S. territorial waters, but at present they are hunted around Antarctica, Norway, Japan, and Iceland. The worldwide population certainly numbers in the hundreds of thousands, but many local populations have been seriously depleted.

Minke whales are comparatively small true whales and very secretive in their behavior. Compared to other whales, they spend little time at the surface, and their blow is tiny and inconspicuous. (Stanley M. Minasian)

HUMPBACK WHALE
Megaptera novaeangliae

Humpback whales are creatures of the world's oceans, not just Hawaiian waters, though they generally prefer nearshore and near-island habitats for both feeding and breeding. The name derives from their habit of raising the back around the dorsal fin high above the water before diving. Their lifestyle is characterized by extensive migration toward temperate and polar latitudes for feeding in summer months, and toward tropical or near-tropical latitudes in winter for breeding. During the latter time, little or no feeding takes place while the energetic gambols of the mating game are sustained for several months by the whales' blubber. The waters around the Hawaiian Islands are a favored place for the breeding and calving activities of these whales in the North Pacific Ocean.

Beginning in late November, a few humpback whales appear around some of the Hawaiian Islands to sing their plaintive songs in underwater serenade, awaiting the arrival of others of their kind. By January, humpbacks are arriving in increasing numbers; and by February, a thousand or more of these playful giants are swimming around the islands and offshore banks, mooing and crooning and chasing one another about excitedly. The calves resulting from the previous year's meeting are born in January and early February. After birth they grow astonishingly fast, more than doubling their weight before March, when the migratory procession begins toward the feeding areas in higher latitudes.

Humpback whales are huge animals—an adult is easily as large as a bus, but much heavier. A forty-five-foot-long humpback whale once weighed in at 45 tons, and some are bigger than that! Most, however, are 35 to 45 feet in length and weigh about one ton per foot. Though gigantic in size, humpback whales pose no threat to humans. In fact, the chances of even seeing a whale in its natural habitat by chance are remote indeed. Yet the burgeoning desire to see them has contributed to the new recreation of whale watching, and nowhere is it more popular and evident than in Hawaii. Cruises to watch humpback whales are offered in Hawaii from January through April, when one would be virtually assured of seeing one or more of these wondrous creatures up close.

The mating technique of humpback whales is not completely understood—in fact, their mating has never been observed. However, they are not monogamous; that much is known, and popular myths to the contrary should be dispelled. Numerous males romp and chase after each female, jostling for position, scuffling and bumping each other in splashy frenzy. At some point—whether during or after these scuffles, no one knows—mating occurs. Eleven to twelve months later, back in these same waters, the females who were objects of these amorous chases each give birth to a 13-foot-long, two-ton calf. Usually the new mother is exempt from the vigorous mating chases while she is nursing, but she does undergo a postpartum estrus ("heat") about one month after birthing, at which time both she and her calf may be chased around. As a result, some females may be taxed with having a calf every year for several years in succession. This is a big tax, because not only does the mother develop another two-ton fetus in her womb during the ensuing year, she also must supply her calf with 100 pounds of milk per day for about five to seven months until it is weaned. The calf has by then doubled its length and quintupled its birth weight to 27 feet and 10 tons! A calf a year, though, is maximum biological productivity for a female humpback—more typically, she has a calf every second or third year during her breeding life, and less often in later years.

Sexual maturity may be attained as early as age four in both sexes, and the natural lifespan is well in excess of 30 years. In the past, age has been surmised from specimens taken during whaling operations; specifically the ear canal of baleen whales (filter feeders; of which the humpback is one species) fills with earwax be-

16

Humpback whales make excellent mothers, guarding their babies closely through the first months of their lives seldom allowing the infants to leave their sides. (James D. Watt)

cause there is no external ear opening. As the whale grows, the ear canal and its accumulating "wax plug" grow with it, the latter in layers much like growth rings of trees. In this way, some humpbacks taken off Australia have been determined to be 58 years old; but since the whales died unnaturally, nobody really knows what their lifespan might have been. Age tables constructed from the catch of many whales suggest, however, that life span is normally 30 to 40 years. Current research involving photo-identification of individual humpback whales in Hawaii and elsewhere is yielding a great deal of information about their migratory movements, population status, associations, behavior, and growth that points to a knowledge in future years that will be more complete than for any other species of large whale. All this will come about without killing or harming a single whale, simply because of the cooperative efforts of many dedicated researchers and whale enthusiasts who are compiling the necessary identification photographs.

The genus name, *Megaptera*, means "big wing", referring to the

Humpbacks are named for the tendency to arch their backs prior to a lengthy, deep dive. Note the white color pattern on the underside of the flukes, which is as unique to an individual humpback as fingerprints are to a human. (Thomas Johnson)

enormous forelimbs or flippers of these ponderous looking whales. There is one humpback whale species recognized worldwide, *M. novaeangliae*, though others have been proposed and used from time to time in reference to animals from geographically distinct populations. Anatomically there are no significant differences between the populations described, so most often they have all been referred to as one species that was originally described from New England (hence, *novaeangliae*).

All over the world, humpback whales have been exploited excessively by commercial whalers because of their accessibility nearshore and their habitual return to specific areas. Most populations were truly decimated in this century, leaving only five to ten percent of the original stock surviving. In the North Pacific Ocean, many thousands of these whales were taken from feeding and breeding areas, and it has been estimated that fewer than 1,000

18

remained there when hunting was halted by international treaty in 1964. The breeding population which returns to Hawaii in winter months now numbers several thousand whales, most of which apparently feed near Alaska. In spite of their apparent recovery, humpbacks are still completely protected from hunting or harassment and remain on the Endangered Species List.

The islands of Hawaii offer the most accessible places in the world to see humpbacks on their winter range, particularly in the so-called "four-island area" near Maui, Lanai, Kahoolawe, and Molokai. The largest concentrations of humpback whales in Hawaiian waters can be found on Penguin Bank west of Molokai, but the water is usually too rough there for comfortable whale watching. As the population around Hawaii increases, it will not be uncommon to see one or more of these playful giants cruising off Waikiki in season—making for exciting additional entertainment on a dinner cruise.

RIGHT WHALE
Eubalaena glacialis

Right whales are not usually thought of as common around Hawaii, but in the winter of 1979 one did appear and was photographed frolicking with humpback whales near the island of Maui. The photographs taken of this animal are particularly remarkable in that they document one of the few sightings of this species in the North Pacific in this century, following their near-total decimation by Yankee whalers in the last one. From 1804 to 1876 American whalers alone killed 193,522 right whales worldwide, estimated at 95 to 97 percent of the total world population. It is unlikely that right whales ever regularly wintered near Hawaii, but one was reported taken by whalers in Hawaiian waters in 1866.

Right whales are typically seen in temperate and subpolar waters. While some nomadic individuals will travel across vast expanses of ocean, as we have seen, to tropical climates like Hawaii, most right whales travel in small feeding groups of two to three individuals in high latitudes until late fall. At that time they gather into larger herds, known as "gams" to early whalers, and move toward the temperate parts of their range.

The breeding and calving season commences with the arrival of winter, but the location of any North Pacific breeding grounds remains a mystery. Presumably, they move toward warmer waters and better weather, but a thorough search by early whalers did not reveal their secret hideaways. In some oceans, where remnant herds survived, breeding and calving grounds have been found in recent years, in bays and coastal waters which are now protected (for example, Peninsula Valdez in Argentina and Campbell Island

Newborn great whales look like miniatures of their parents, both in shape and color. This right whale calf displays the collosites which are unique to its species. The pattern is also unique to individuals. (Ricardo Mandojana)

Like all whale species, right whales are solicitous of their young. Newborn are almost always found alongside their mother for security and protection. (Jen and Des Bartlett, courtesy Survival Anglia Limited)

21

in New Zealand). Perhaps if the beleagured individuals of the North Pacific ever recover enough to form herds, their secret grounds will be found and protected. It is currently estimated that only 100 to 200 right whales remain in the entire North Pacific and adjacent seas, and there is no indication that their number is increasing.

Right whales grow to about 60 feet and are exceptionally full-bodied, weighing 80 to 100 or more tons. More often, they reach 40 to 50 feet in length and weigh a ton or more per foot. Females are larger than males by several feet and thousands of pounds at sexual maturity, which is estimated to occur around age 8 to 10. Gestation takes about one year, and calves are weaned by about one year. During the first year they take some solid food (euphausid shrimps, primarily, in the North Pacific); and they grow from a birth size of 18 feet to about 26 feet, increasing many times in weight. The calving interval is estimated at around three years, and life span is probably around 50 years.

Right whales are friendly and extremely inquisitive animals, often approaching vessels close enough to be photographed in great detail. (Birgit Winning)

Sperm whale (Robert L. Pitman)

SPERM WHALE
Physeter macrocephalus

Sperm whales formed the basis of the American whale fishery in the last two centuries, and their form is the one that usually comes to mind when we think of whales. Whalers took other species, but the mainstay of the industry was the toothy leviathan of *Moby Dick* fame. The New England whaling ports of Nantucket and New Bedford sent hundreds of ships and thousands of men each year out across the vast oceans in search of these whales to render them into lamp oil and candles. The voyages lasted many years, and they were often lucrative for the boat owners but seldom for their crews. The best one could hope for aboard a sperm whaler was adventure and travel to faraway places and exotic ports and, if all went well, to come home again with a few coins in the pocket after the ship's bills were paid. The work was grueling and dangerous, not least because in their death throes, these whales would occasionally bite and thrash boats and crews to oblivion. It was an exciting business and attracted generations of men to sea in pursuit of whales; and it supplied the basis for much of what we know today about the distribution and habits of these enormous animals.

Sperm whales keep to waters 1,000 or more fathoms deep as a rule. Exceptions to this are adult males, which travel in groups by themselves and may feed on or near shallow banks at high latitudes, and the occasional herds which may follow prey species or currents close to shore. These herds sometimes strand in catastrophic fashion, usually on gently sloping sand beaches. Sperm whales are gregarious, forming herds of dozens to hundreds in their favorite habitats, which were known to the whalers as ''grounds''. These grounds were known and charted according to the seasons and migrations of the whales, and they yielded several hundred thousand of these valuable creatures to American whalers. One of

Gliding slowly beneath the surface in Hawaiian waters, these 50-foot long sperm whales reveal their strange form: tiny flippers, a box-shaped head, and rippled skin. (Carl Spencer)

Overleaf: the first photograph ever taken of a whale calf suckling. This calf is upside down under its mother. The photographer captured this sperm whale family on film while photographing marlin off Hawaii's Kona Coast. (Carl Spencer)

the famous areas was the Lahaina ground, perhaps not so much for the whales it yielded as for the rest and recreation it offered the crews during whaling voyages.

Sperm whales did and do appear in the channels around Maui and the other Hawaiian Islands, particularly in the late spring through fall. Most of those seen occur in small "nursery" herds comprised of females and their calves, subadults, and the occasional adult male. When the adult males are present in herds of this polygynous species, they are known as "harem" herds. Other herds usually found in higher latitudes are "bachelor" herds, comprised of sexually mature (but socially immature) males, and solitary individuals or breeding males, called "bulls". This species exhibits sexual and social segregation to a remarkable degree, with males ranging as far as polar waters, while females and young seldom venture beyond tropical and temperate zones.

Sperm whales which are seen in and around Hawaiian waters

25

Sperm whales (Carl Spencer)

are preponderantly in nursery and harem herds. They usually form small groups which may be related in some way and are usually very tolerant of vessel intrusion. The usual behavior of sperm whales is to dive for up to an hour and then spend about ten minutes at the surface, breathing (blowing) at ten- to twenty-second intervals. Occasionally these whales will be boisterous or playful, breaching or chasing each other around; but usually they just swim slowly, breathe, and then lift their flukes in the air to signal the start of another long, deep dive.

Sperm whales breed throughout the year, although the peak of activity occurs in winter. Gestation is 17 months, and the nursing period typically lasts over a year. Usually there is a year of rest for a female after weaning her calf, so the reproductive interval is about four years. The age of most toothed whales, including sperm whales, is inferred from "growth rings" in the teeth, which accumulate much like growth rings in a tree. (The growth ceases in old age in whales, however, and the age estimates may therefore be too low.) Males may also become sexually mature around age eleven or twelve, but for reasons yet unknown, they are not socially acceptable to the mature females until they are about age twenty-five, and they segregate into bachelor herds during this interim period. We can surmise that this segregation is good evolutionary

Sperm whales are one of the deepest-diving whales, feeding on organisms living up to two miles from the surface. Prior to a lengthy dive, the flukes are often raised high into the air. (Kenneth C. Balcomb III)

Sperm whales are oddities in the animal kingdom, for the nostril (blowhole) is shifted to the extreme left front side of the head. (Kenneth C. Balcomb III)

strategy in terms of exploiting prey species (males and females tend to feed separately, and so do not compete for resources), but the interesting question remains—how did it develop?

Sperm whales are polygynous; that is, the typical breeding pattern is for a single male to breed with numerous females (a "harem") which is defended from other males. Polygyny in animals is typically accompanied by obvious differences between males and females, and in this case the differences are extreme: mature males grow to 60 feet in length, while females rarely reach 40 feet.

PYGMY SPERM WHALE
Kogia breviceps

DWARF SPERM WHALE
Kogia simus

Rarely identified at sea, pygmy and dwarf sperm whales look much alike, although the pygmy (at 10 feet and 800 pounds mature size) is larger than the dwarf (8 feet and 400 pounds). The pygmy sperm whale has a smaller dorsal fin than the dwarf sperm whale, and it is placed further back on the body. That is about the only way one can tell them apart. Both species have a squarish head and underslung lower jaw, like their large namesake kin, the sperm whale; and both range throughout temperate and tropical oceans worldwide, generally offshore in deep water. Both are squid eaters, for which they dive deep and for long durations. Members of both species have stranded in the Hawaiian Islands.

Coloration is dark grey on top and lighter grey below, with a bracket-shaped light grey streak behind the eye, giving the appearance of gills. They do not have gills, of course; rather, they breathe air like all other cetaceans, exhaling a little puff of misty air that is difficult to see.

This photo of a dwarf sperm whale that beached itself and was later brought to Marineland of Florida shows the underslung jaw, squarish head, and gill-like coloration behind the eye. (Courtesy Marineland of Florida)

In the channels between the islands, one might encounter these little whales individually or in small groups, in waters 6,000 feet or more deep. The typical sighting is brief and of only one individual, but reliable observers have reported groups of half a dozen or so, some displaying curiosity about a passing ship. Along the East Coast of the United States, between New York and Florida, dozens of these little whales wash ashore each year, many showing evidence of having been hit by ships. Perhaps their curiosity gets the best of them and they get too close to vessels underway. They do swim rather lethargically, unlike the spirited dolphins.

Virtually nothing is known about the life history and status of either the pygmy or the dwarf sperm whale. Their offshore habits make them difficult to study, and there are no regular fisheries for these species. They do not often entangle in fishing gear, so we must rely upon stranded specimens for our information. Usually, stranded specimens have not been analyzed in sufficient detail to fill in the basic information about the age at sexual maturity, the reproductive rate, life span, etc. It is estimated, however, that gestation lasts about one year, and calves are born in spring.

These pygmy sperm whales can be distinguished from their dwarf sperm whale look-alikes by their smaller dorsal fin set further back on the body. In nearly all other respects, the two species are identical both in looks and distribution. (Robert L. Pitman)

BAIRD'S BEAKED WHALE
Berardius bairdii

While it would be exceedingly unlikely to find any Baird's beaked whales around the main islands of Hawaii, these large toothed whales do occur just a few hundred miles north of the archipelago. Indeed, some of their favorite haunts are around the Emperor Seamount chain, whose escarpments extend north and west from the Hawaiian Leeward Islands. There, these bizarre-looking, shy whales gather together in herds from half a dozen up to several score and dive to great depths to feed upon the squid and bottom fishes which comprise their diet. They also favor the steep continental slopes from Japan around the North Pacific Aleutian rim to California. The overall distribution of Baird's beaked whales ranges from about 32 degrees latitude to the ice edge in the Bering and Okhotsk Seas. They are not found outside the North Pacific and adjacent seas.

Because of this distribution, Baird's beaked whales have been described as "antitropical" creatures. Their occurrence in tropical regions is considered unusual and is probably related to habits and seasonal abundance of prey species which live at great depths. Just as there can be snow at high elevations even in tropical latitudes (for instance, on Mauna Loa and Mauna Kea), ocean water becomes much cooler with depth, until at about 3,000 feet it is slightly above freezing almost everywhere. In other words, within about half a mile of the surface the oceans are vitually polar worldwide, even at the equator. Deep diving whales spend most of the day in polar waters even when the surface waters are warm. For this reason, it may be possible to see Baird's beaked whales around the Hawaiian Islands.

Baird's beaked whales attain lengths up to 42 feet, but 35 to 38 feet is the norm, with a body weight of about 10 tons. Females are slightly larger than males—unusual among toothed whales—and they segregate from males at certain times or in certain areas. (See chapter on sperm whales for a description of such a social structure.) Their external appearance is similar to a greatly overgrown bottlenosed dolphin, but with a relatively tiny dorsal fin set two thirds of the way back, behind a troughlike longitudinal depression created by massively bulging muscles. Coloration is dark grey to black or brownish black, depending upon the whale's age and the extent of encrustation by diatoms. Young whales are lighter than adults and are relatively unscarred, while adults become heavily crisscrossed with white scars inflicted by the teeth of their fellows.

As with other beaked whales, these animals have very few teeth—only four, all on the lower jaw. The lower jaw protrudes

The bulbous forehead and protruding teeth on the extended lower jaw identify this Baird's beaked whale, photographed in the North Pacific Ocean. (Kenneth C. Balcomb III)

Baird's beaked whales are frequently observed in groups of a dozen or more, rising simultaneously to breathe and often following a herd leader. (Painting by Larry Foster)

markedly beyond the upper, and it bears two prominent fist-sized triangular teeth at its tip, with two smaller flat acorn-shaped teeth further back. The whales jut these teeth forward with a thrust of the chin as they surface to breathe.

The "blow" is low and bushy but quite noticeable at a distance in calm seas. Because these whales are gregarious and come up for breath simultaneously between their normal twenty- to forty-minute dives, a group is usually first noted by the staccato appearance of these white puffs at intervals of thirty seconds or so for about five minutes, until all the whales have recharged their oxygen supplies for another dive. They are characteristically shy of vessels, but if a group comes up near a boat accidentally, they will nervously stay near the surface and breathe if the boat does not race toward them.

Sexual maturity is estimated to occur between 8 and 10 years age, and physical maturity occurs after 20 years. The natural life-span is unknown but is probably rather long, perhaps about as long as ours. Life for these whales is apparently tough, especially for

Baird's beaked whales travel in groups, spending a great deal of time below the surface feeding. On the surface however, they are often curious enough to approach unobtrusive boats. (Robert L. Pitman)

adults. In addition to the numerous and evidently serious wounds they inflict upon one another (for reasons unknown), many of these whales bear scars left by killer whales, and virtually all of them bear scars left by sharks. It is surmised that the scars inflicted by their own kind have something to do with the mating game, in which both sexes take a beating.

Gestation lasts 17 months, and the newborn whales are relatively large, about 15 feet long and weighing over a ton. The nursing period is unknown, as is the calving interval. In fact, almost everything about the lifestyle of these whales is unknown, except that they seem to appear in the summer and disappear in the winter throughout their range. Apparently, they move offshore in winter months, but nobody knows where.

BLAINVILLE'S BEAKED WHALE
Mesoplodon densirostris

Blainville's beaked whales (also known as dense-beaked whales), one of nature's rarest curiosities, are found in tropical and subtropical seas. Until a few years ago, the existence of these creatures was known only from bones, and those could only be identified and appreciated by a cetacean specialist. In recent years, however, a few of these bizarre little whales have been recognized and photographed alive in Hawaiian waters. Among other reasons, their penchant for traveling in deep waters makes them more common in Hawaii than anywhere else in the world, for these islands drop off precipitously to depths beyond 1,000 fathoms.

Blainville's beaked whales are deep divers, feeding on squid and fish found in deep waters. They stay down 10 to 40 minutes at a time and come up only to breathe (blow) a few times before diving again. They are about 14 feet long when fully mature, and their coloration is silver-grey to brown on top and lighter grey to white underneath, with small oval white scars and scratches all over the body like pockmarks. Young animals are lighter in color and less marked. The dorsal fin is small (about 10 inches high) and placed well back on the body. The identifying behavior of the genus is that upon surfacing the chin and rostrum are thrust vigorously above the water and then rocked back down underwater as the back and dorsal fin appear. Female and young Blainville's beaked whales have an upward sweep of the mouth like a smile that, if noticed, will help identify them. But the real telling feature of the species is found in the adult male: from the middle of the lower jaw there protrude two large teeth, (one on each side), sticking straight up above the head like little spiky antlers. They cannot be missed. As if to accentuate their bizarre appearance, these teeth are usually encrusted with stalked barnacles and vermin of various kind,

Blainville's beaked whales are known to travel in small numbers, as indicated by this group of three photographed several miles off the main island of Hawaii's Kona coast. [James D. Watt/Ron Evans]

which make them appear for all the world like little yellow-orange bonnets. Of course they are not mere decoration—they are the daggers responsible for the wounds and scars seen on these animals. These are very unusual animals whose habits are largely unknown.

As of 1972, there were 26 specimens of this species in various museums around the world. None had been found alive. Since that time, several more specimens have washed up on various beaches of the world, and a number of living animals have been photographed and documented. Nothing is known of the size of the population, except that they are uncommon throughout their range.

A rare glimpse of an uncommon animal, this underwater photograph of a Blainville's beaked whale displays its strange body form and coloration. (James D. Watt/Ron Evans)

When male Blainville's beaked whales are not involved in fights for mating rights, barnacles may grow on the tips of the teeth. Two teeth erupt through the gums in the lower jaws only in the males. (Randall S. Wells)

CUVIER'S BEAKED WHALE
Ziphius cavirostris

The most widely distributed of the enigmatic family of beaked whales (Ziphiidae), Cuvier's beaked whales, also known as goosebeaked whales, occur year-round in Hawaiian waters, generally offshore in deep water. Little is known about their habits, except that they dine on squid and deep-sea fishes in all but polar seas. They often travel singly or in small groups, and when they strand it is almost always singly (in marked contrast to pilot whales, for example). They are not particularly shy of vessels (indeed, they will occasionally approach closely for inspection), but they dive for long periods—up to forty minutes—and their "blow" is rather inconspicuous. Hence, they often go unnoticed, despite being up to 23 feet long.

The coloration of Cuvier's beaked whales is extremely variable, with much of the variation due to age. Young individuals are acorn brown over most of the body, with lighter color on the head and underside. Older individuals, especially males, become much lighter, to the point that the forward part of the body may be white. As in the case of all beaked whales, there is increasing tooth scarring after sexual maturity, when long paired tooth rakes may be seen all over. The skin is also pocked with small oval scars, which are probably the work of cookie-cutter sharks (see the chapter on Baird's beaked whale for their description); and sometimes there are bites from other cetaceans. Adult pigmentation, aside from this scarring and lightening, may vary from acorn brown to gunmetal blue. The overall result is often a quite beautiful pattern, with no two individuals looking the same.

In keeping with the family characteristic of having few teeth, Cuvier's beaked whales have only two, both projecting forward and upward from the tip of the lower jaw. These are small in females,

40

Cuvier's beaked whales are found around all the Hawaiian islands, in deeper offshore waters. Although sightings are rare, they occur often enough to establish the animals' year-round presence. (Painting by Larry Foster)

about the size of an acorn, and they rarely erupt from the gum; but in males they may be much bigger than a man's thumb and protrude an inch or so. The forehead bulges slightly and tapers toward the snout, without a crease or demarcation, to form a "beak". The profile is similar to that of a goose from the eyes forward. Under the chin, there is a V-shaped pair of grooves which extend back under the throat, another characteristic of all beaked whales.

The body is robust and thinner from side to side than from top to bottom, with girth being about 60 percent of the total length. The dorsal fin, located two thirds of the way back on the body is curved backwards and relatively small (about 9 to 12 inches tall) for a 16- to 22-foot whale. The flukes are broad (about 25 percent of the body length, or 5 feet for a 20-foot whale) and pointed at the tips, without a median notch. The flippers, on the other hand, are spatulate and small (about 10 percent of the body length, or 2 feet for a 20-foot whale). They are usually tucked into "pockets", (slight depressions on the lower chest) when the whales are swimming.

The chin is often thrust above the water when the whales surface to breathe, but the flukes are almost never raised. At the surface, these whales seem to lurch through the water, but underwater their movements are graceful and fluid. In recent years, a few divers in Hawaiian waters have been lucky enough to see and photograph these whales underwater (see accompanying photograph). They are not aggressive toward people, as far as we know.

The details of life history are a bit sketchy. Birth size is about 9 feet. Sexual maturity occurs in females by the time they are 18 to 20 feet in length and in males by about 18 feet; the age at those lengths is unknown. Based on growth layers in the teeth, the lifespan may exceed 35 years. The gestation period is unknown, as is the nursing period, but young whales may take solid food by the time they are 11 feet long. Very few weights have been recorded, as these whales are not usually caught in commercial fisheries. One stranded 19-foot male weighed in at 5,700 pounds, and it was said to look undernourished.

Sightings of Cuvier's beaked whales are not uncommon in Hawaiian waters. This is the only known full-body underwater photograph of a free-swimming Cuvier's beaked whale. It was taken off the Kona Coast while three animals spent more than five minutes swimming near the photographer's boat. (James D. Watt)

Hawaiian spinner dolphin (Randall S. Wells)

SHORT-FINNED PILOT WHALE
Globicephala macrorhynchus

Pilot whales are among the most ubiquitous and numerous of all cetaceans, being found worldwide in all but polar seas. Each population seems to possess its own stereotypic physical characteristics, but most cetologists agree that there are only two basic species: the short-finned pilot whale (*Globicephala macrorhynchus*) in tropical latitudes, and the long-finned pilot whale (*Globicephala melaena*) in temperate and subpolar latitudes. In the North Pacific, the short-finned pilot whale ranges far into temperate zones, and they represent the numerically dominant species of pilot whale.

Those that occur year-round in Hawaiian waters are of this short-finned species, typically traveling in herds of 20 to 40, though aggregations of hundreds may sometimes be seen. They are found in the deep waters of channels between the main islands, like Alenuihaha Channel, and offshore; here and there, they may rest in groups at the surface (''logging'') on nice days. At such times, they can rather easily be approached by boats, but as with all cetaceans, a slow and respectful approach is more likely to give a good view than a rapid approach or chase, and it is more law-abiding. (See introduction.) When pilot whales are traveling, or are frightened or hurt, they all stay together no matter what happens. This ''epimelitic'' behavior has led to spectacularly tragic mass strandings in various parts of the world, often reported as suicides. It is doubtful that these mass strandings are the result of a death wish; more likely the whales (or, more precisely, the leaders at the time) simply erred in a confusing situation of shifting tides, stormy weather, or sandy shores. Maybe their internal compass simply failed. There are locations with magnetic anomalies or unusual beach characteristics where such strandings are relatively frequent (on a scale of years).

Pilot whales are very social animals, with close family interactions. Here, in the crystal clear Hawaiian waters, a group of adults swims with a newborn calf. (Jacki Kilbride)

Fortunately, the populations are quite large and the reproductive rates are high, so these losses, although tragic indeed, are inconsequential to the species in the long run. Indeed, mass strandings of pilot whales appear in the fossil record, and they probably will continue when humans are found only in the fossil record.

The mating system is polygynous (a male has several mates), and the breeding is seasonal, with a birthrate peak in July and August. A single calf about 55 inches long is born after almost 15 months gestation, and it is nursed for a minimum of about two years. Calves of older cows may be nursed for considerably longer than this. Females mature at 7 to 12 years, produce an average of four to five calves in their lifetimes, and have their last calf before age 40, even though they may live up to 63 years. In contrast, males live only to about 46 years of age and probably continue to be capable of reproduction until death. In males, puberty begins at 7 to 17 years of age and social maturity at an average of 17 years.

Males may migrate between herds after weaning, but females probably stay with their mother's herd for life. This implies that breeding herds are essentially matrilineal kinship groups (as is the case for elephants) that grow continually, like a tree with maternal branches.

Pilot whales are very nomadic in their habits, but some pods, or family units, may return seasonally to favorite haunts. They primarily eat squid, but they will eat herring, mackerel, and other species of fish as well as invertebrates. Some rogues have been known to eat other small cetaceans, as do the closely related killer whales. They are not aggressive toward people without provocation.

Pilot whales are often seen "logging" on the surface of the water; that is, moving very slowly and exposing only the top of their heads and their dorsal fins. (Robert L. Pitman)

FALSE KILLER WHALE
Pseudorca crassidens

Residents of tropical and temperate seas worldwide, false killer whales are gregarious animals that travel in groups of half a dozen to several hundred individuals, often in association with other cetacean species. They roam the seas in search of large fish (mahi mahi, for instance) and squid, lingering in areas where such prey is abundant. They have been known to take fish and bait off fishing lines, thereby earning the wrath of both sport and commercial fishermen. Adults range in size from 16 to 19 feet and weigh 2,000 to 3,000 pounds, with the females slightly smaller. Coloration is almost entirely glossy black, with a lighter grey-to-white swath in the middle of the chest and belly and a hint of smoky grey outlining the characteristic fatty forehead. The forehead bulges in front of the upper lip without a break and is smoothly rounded with a slight flattening on the top, like the toe of a regulation military shoe. The large sickle-shaped dorsal fin is located almost precisely at the midpoint of the body. The flippers are large and have a forward bulge, or "elbow", that give them the appearance of being installed backwards.

False killer whales are energetic creatures that will ride the bow waves of ships like the overgrown dolphins they are. They often "porpoise" as they travel along, at speeds up to 15 knots, leaping forward almost completely out of the water. They have been caught and trained for display in marine parks where they have proved remarkably tractable and hardy. One has been kept for many years at Sea Life Park on Oahu, where its featured display is an awesome 25-foot vertical leap to take a fish from the hand of its trainer. This aquarium animal offers the best chance of seeing this species in Hawaii.

In the waters around Hawaii, false killer whales may be found infrequently during all seasons of the year. They typically feed in deep water on species of fish that humans like to eat too, so your best chance to see them in the wild is to accompany Hawaiian fishing boats. Other similar species may be observed (melon-headed whale and pygmy killer whale), but false killer whales are one and a half to two times as big, with that distinctive rounded forehead. The only comparably sized species for which they might be mistaken is the pilot whale, although this species has a much more bulbous forehead, a dorsal fin further forward on the body, and a much less vigorous swimming behavior (e.g., pilot whales do not typically "porpoise" as they swim).

Sexual maturity is attained between the age of 8 and 14, when females are about 12.5 to 13 feet long, and males slightly longer.

False killer whales are very active at the surface, often raising their head and flippers out of the water as they travel. (Robert L. Pitman)

Friendly and curious, false killer whales often approach divers closely underwater. (Christopher Newbert)

Gestation is variously reported to take between 12 and 15.5 months, and lactation is estimated to last 18 months. Nothing is known about the calving interval, but we may surmise by comparison of like species that it is two to four years. Nothing is known about maximum life span in this species.

False killer whales are large members of the dolphin family, Delphinidae. They are hunted in some parts of the world for their meat and oil, but nowhere are they particularly abundant, and their occurence is unpredictable. They are not considered endangered but are afforded protection in U.S. territorial waters, as are all marine mammals. False killer whales are occasionally caught on long-line fishing gear, and occasionally they strand *en masse*, sometimes causing the death of the entire herd. The size of the population worldwide is not known.

The large bump on the leading edge of the flippers distinguishes false killer whales from pygmy killer whales, melon-headed whales, and pilot whales. (Robert L. Pitman)

MELON-HEADED WHALE
Peponocephala electra

A pelagic species which is found in the world's tropical and sub-tropical regions, melon-headed whales, also known as "many-toothed blackfish", are gregarious creatures that typically travel in large herds of a hundred to a thousand or more individuals, often in the company of other cetacean species. They are generally wary of vessels and will group together and flee in a frothy shoal of shallow leaps which obscures their identity (see also Fraser's Dolphin, pg. 95). On rare occasions, when in small or widely dispersed groups which may be feeding, some individuals may be approached to see their identifying characteristics.

Melon-headed whales grow to about 8 feet in length and 350 to 400 pounds. When fully grown they are mostly black, with a small white blotch on the chin which often extends to the tip and a cloudy grey swath tapering from the throat area to a point between the flippers. The chest and flanks are slightly less dark than the rest of the body, lending the appearance of a darker head and cape around the dorsal fin. The head is distinctly wedge-shaped, tapering forward to an indistinct "beak", with the line of the mouth sweeping slightly upward. As the alias implies, there are numerous teeth (20 to 25) in each upper and lower jaw. The flippers are long, slender, and pointed at the tips; the dorsal fin is tall, thin and distinctly curved.

Little is known of the natural history of these shy creatures. There is the suggestion from stranded animals that they may have a breeding season in the spring. Newborn animals are about 3.5 feet and become sexually mature at about 7.5 feet. The diet consists principally of squid and a variety of small fish species. Herds of melon-headed whales are found around Hawaiian waters all year long.

Melon-headed whales are average-sized members of the dolphin

Close observation of melon-headed whales reveals their pointed flippers and flukes, unlike the rounded forms of their cousins, the pygmy killer whales. (Howard Hall)

family, Delphinidae. The population status is unknown, but this species is considered rare throughout most of its range, though reportedly abundant near Cebo Island in the Philippines. This species is not hunted or the object of direct fisheries; but it is occasionally taken incidentally in purse seine fisheries for tuna in the eastern tropical Pacific, and it is sometimes purposely taken in fisheries in coastal Japan.

Rare even in their known range, melon-headed whales travel in fairly large herds and occasionally leap clear of the water to expose their strange form and subtle color pattern. (Edward Shallenberger)

PYGMY KILLER WHALE
Feresa attenuata

Pygmy killer whales are found in tropical waters all over the world, and they occur year-round in Hawaii, although not in particular abundance. They are gregarious animals that travel in herds numbering from a few to fifty or more, and they are usually shy of vessels. In Hawaii their preferred diet is mahi mahi (a tarpon-like fish also called Dolphin or Dorado), squid, and tuna, which are typically found in deep offshore waters; and they have been known to attack other small cetaceans. Probably the best opportunity to see some of these little whales would be offshore where commercial and sport fishing takes place; keep a sharp eye our for their sharply pointed black dorsal fins.

In captivity, pygmy killer whales elicit fear reactions from other dolphins and sometimes from their trainers as they charge and bite and snap their jaws in anger. These little whales received their name by virtue of skull and teeth similarities with the larger killer whales (see pg. 56); and they seem bent on living up to a feisty image. In the wild, they have allowed divers to swim among them on occasion without behaving aggressively. On one occasion, a diver was ''offered'' a piece of mahi mahi by one of these whales; but when accepted, the whales' eyes reddened and it appeared so angry that the gift was returned.

On close examination, the coloration of these whales is bluish-black over much of the body with a noticeably darker, somewhat brownish cape region around and forward of the dorsal fin. The forehead is bluntly rounded with no hint of a beak or rostrum, and the lips are white in a thin margin along the mouth line, sometimes beginning with a little ''goatee'' at the tip of the chin. The underside is splashed with light grey between the flippers, shading to white in the umbilical and genital area. These whales grow to about

53

*Pygmy killer whales are very social animals and often travel in large herds.
(James D. Watt)*

9 feet in length and 375 pounds when fully mature, with females
being slightly smaller; a newborn is about 3 feet in length. The
sickle-shaped dorsal fin is large (about one foot tall), located mid-
length, and sharply pointed at the tip. The flippers are of moder-
ate size, rounded at the tip, and distinctly rounded on the leading
edge.

Pygmy killer whales are true creatures of the open tropical seas,
with virtually unlimited passport to all oceans. In some respects
their name is misleading, because they are really average-sized
members of the dolphin family, Delphinidae. The pygmy killer
"whale" appellation probably derives from the earliest descriptive
accounts of skeletons, which bear some similarity to those of true
killer whales (i.e., a tooth count of 22 to 26 in the upper jaw and

16 to 22 in the lower). The population status is unknown: these little whales are not the objects of a direct fishery, so there have been no attempts to estimate their numbers. Along with all other marine mammals, they are protected in the economic zone extending 200 miles around U.S. territory, but this forms a minuscule portion of their oceanic habitat. Perhaps the biggest threat to them and all their kin derives from the expanding drift gill-net fishery in the Pacific Ocean, which promises to soon cover much of the surface waters from North America to Asia. Unfortunately, whales and dolphins must come to the surface to breathe, and when they do so the smaller species often become entangled in the tough monofilament mesh of these nets and drown. Not being the objects of the fisheries, their carcasses are usually thrown back into the ocean with little concern for the effect of such mayhem.

Filmed through the underwater bow window of a research ship, the strange configuration of the pygmy killer whale is evident. The rainbow effect is caused by the sun's reflection off the plexiglass window. (Robert L. Pitman)

KILLER WHALE
Orcinus orca

Not to be confused with any of the smaller species in the preceding descriptions, killer whales are large panda-pigmented predators that simply have no peers. Unfortunately, they do not show up in Hawaiian waters very often, so there is little chance to see one here. Any killer whales which might appear off Hawaii are members of a natural population whose territory covers the vast expanse of ocean between Asia and America, and between the two poles. The species is found worldwide.

Killer whales typically travel in ''pods'' or clans of related individuals which may number from a few to fifty or more. An average-sized pod contains maybe a dozen whales; six adult females, and six sub-adults and/or calves is a typical configuration. However, individuals, pairs, and trios are not uncommon. Likewise, aggregations of several pods have been reported to number in the hundreds or even thousands of individuals; but these are exceptions and only occur in higher latitudes. In Hawaiian waters, the average pod or smaller group is all that is likely to be seen, and then only rarely.

Despite their name, humans have nothing to fear from killer whales in the wild. We are usually interesting to them but probably do not taste very good; furthermore, we are much less available than their natural prey, which is any living thing in the ocean bigger than a small shrimp. Killer whales in general have very peaceful attitudes toward us, sometimes tolerating our rather audicious intrusions into their realm and at other times easily avoiding us al-

Why killer whales breach is not understood, although it has been suggested the resulting loud splash marks their location, or that it gives the animals a viewing advantage. (Olga von Ziegesar)

together. But they do so always with elegance and never with malice.

This is not necessarily the case toward their prey. When they are hungry, they kill and eat. If they feel like playing, they may only maim. Sometimes they seem to just beat other animals up a bit. We never give this a thought when the whales are dealing with shrimp, or fish, or squid, but when they bite a dolphin in two or make meatballs out of seals, we call them killers. It has been suggested that such bloodthirsty connotations be avoided and that these whales simply be called "orca" (from the Latin) instead.

Killer whales grow to 30 feet in length, but 25 feet for males and 20 feet for females is more common. Calves are about 8 feet long and 400 pounds at birth. They sexually mature in their teens and live to a ripe old age of 50 or more years. Some may reach a hundred. Their social structure is apparently matrilineal, with mothers and their offspring remaining together throughout their lifetime. When mothers die, sisters may separate and form their own lineal groups. Males apparently stay with their mothers, but may breed outside the group. When mothers die, the males may lose their affinity for the group, to the point of traveling solo or with brothers.

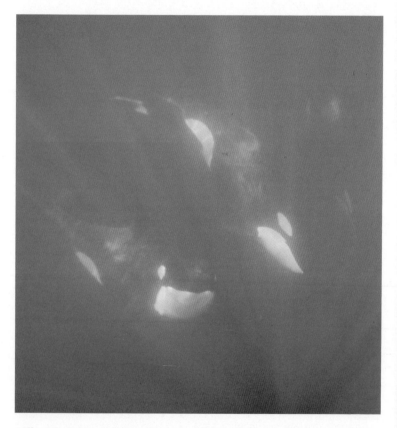

Killer whales feed on just about every large life form in the ocean, yet they are harmless to humans; in fact, they show a marked curiosity toward us. (Bob Talbot/Tony Bernot)

While traveling, killer whales rise slowly and gracefully, often blowing just as they break the surface of the water. (Kenneth C. Balcomb III)

RISSO'S DOLPHIN
Grampus griseus

Surprisingly little is known about Risso's dolphins except that they are widely distributed in the warm waters of the world, typically in small herds of up to twenty individuals. They often travel with other species, including pilot whales, bottlenose dolphins, and northern right whale dolphins, which share their taste for squid. They do not generally go out of their way to frolic with vessels, but there are exceptions. In the early part of this century, an individual named "Pelorous Jack" used to swim regularly in the bow wave of the ferry between the north and south islands of New Zealand, and his arrival was an eagerly awaited part of the trip. Occasionally, other individuals of this species will come over to investigate a vessel, but rarely will an entire herd do so.

Risso's dolphins grow to about 13 feet in length and weigh between 600 and 800 pounds. Sexual maturity occurs at a length of about 9 feet for females and 10 feet for males, at an age of 9 to 12 years, with birthing in summer, and birth size is less than 5 feet. Weaning may occur within a year at a length of about 7 feet. Calving interval and social structure of herds are unknown. Maximum life span is at least 34 years.

The forehead of Risso's dolphins has a distinct melon shape, bulging forward and sloping steeply to the mouth, with no trace of a beak. There is a distinctive and unique vertical crease in the middle of the forehead, and the mouth slopes up sharply. Usually, there are no teeth in the upper jaw and only 3 to 7 pairs in the lower. Body coloration is grey with darker grey to black on the dorsal fin and flippers. Mature animals are often scarred over much of their backs from tooth rakes of others of their kind.

60

Risso's dolphins are often found in the company of other dolphin species. Here a large male, bearing the scars of battle with other males of its kind, joins bottlenose dolphins in riding the bow wave of a research vessel in the tropical Pacific. (Marc Webber)

Risso's dolphins are rare in Hawaiian waters. A large herd was sighted several miles off the Kona coast in February of 1985, swimming with humpback whales, pilot whales, and spotted dolphins. Although attempts were made to film the animals underwater, their shy demeanor thwarted the photographer's efforts.

Risso's dolphins are found in abundance in warm temperate and tropical oceans. They are easily identified at sea by their large white dorsal fin, blunt head, and whitish body. (Robert L. Pitman)

BOTTLENOSE DOLPHIN
Tursiops truncatus

Bottlenose dolphins are without a doubt the best known of all cetaceans by virtue of their inshore habits and playfulness around vessels, and their survival rate and adaptability in captivity.

Bottlenose dolphins become sexually mature around age 11 or 12 and live for more than 30 years. A female produces one offspring every other year, or sometimes every year, with gestation being about 12 months, and nursing extends for as long as twenty months. In captivity, some mothers have produced 10 or more calves. Breeding is apparently promiscuous, but there may be social rules in the wild that we do not yet know about.

Around Hawaii, there are a number of communities of bottlenose dolphins which are mostly resident to particular harbors and coastlines, though some individuals do travel widely. In the deeper waters, the occasional offshore group of dolphins may pass through the interisland channels and forage far beyond sight from shore. To our great delight, however, virtually all of these dolphins will take the time to frolic in the bow wave of vessels underway if they pass near them; and at some point they are usually easily identified. The snout is robust and distinct. The overall size is about 8 to 11 feet, and the coloration is overall grey, often with a darker grey ''cape'' pattern from the forehead to just behind the dorsal fin, and white on the belly. The offshore form is typically darker in appearance than the inshore animals, and it is sometimes less interested in swimming along with boats.

Because inshore bottlenose dolphins tend to establish a foraging range, within which virtually all contacts with their kind are made, they tend to form geographically isolated communities and populations. The result is a rather confusing multiplicity of forms and named species in the worldwide distribution and literature. There are also "offshore bottlenose dolphins" which live an oceanic life and often travel with truly oceanic species, never mixing with their inshore brethren, as far as we know. In the overall scheme, all bottlenose dolphins are much alike and are separable from other species; but they have been a mixed bag for taxonomists since Aristotle, and they remain so today.

It is not known how many bottlenose dolphins may be found around Hawaii. It would be safe to say that a very few thousand of these animals occur around the archipelago, usually in small groups of two to fifteen. Within a few years, many of the resident individuals may be known to dedicated researchers and observers.

Bottlenose dolphin dorsal fins are tall, prominent, falcate (curved to the rear), and rounded at the tip. (Gerard Wellington)

Bottlenose dolphins are the most easily recognized dolphin species. They are found all over the world, avoiding only the higher latitudes. (Gerard Wellington)

ROUGH-TOOTHED DOLPHIN
Steno bredanensis

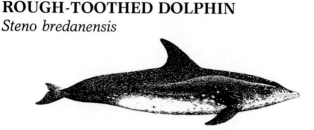

Rough-toothed dolphins are not the most handsome of dolphins—far from it. They look like something out of prehistoric times, with a long toothy snout, bulging eyes, and a complexion which appears pocked with pink and white dots on an otherwise slate-grey skin. They also have tooth scars and scratches all over their skin. The man who caught the first living specimen of this species referred to it as a "calico" or "polka dot" dolphin. In adults, the tip of the rostrum is distinctly white, and there is a splotch of white on the belly. Juveniles are a more even grey overall.

The name "rough-toothed" derives from the unique surface texture of the teeth, which have many fine vertical grooves or "wrinkles" running from the gumline to the tip. These grooves are not easy to see, even with a specimen in hand, but they can be felt; a tooth feels like a fingernail file. Obviously, this characteristic cannot help identify the creature from a boat, but there are external clues. The body size and proportion is much like that of a bottlenose dolphin, but the polka dot coloration is very different. Also distinctive is the snout, which shows no demarcation between the forehead and the rostrum, or beak, lending a "ski-nose" appearance.

Rough-toothed dolphins typically travel around in relatively small groups or three to four individuals, but there may be many such groups in one area. They are relatively common around Hawaii, but their distribution is primarily offshore in waters of 1,000 fathoms or more, so they are usually seen only by deep-sea fishermen or pleasure boaters. A few members of this species have stranded around the Hawaiian Islands, and one as far north as Washington State, but the overall range of this species is predominantly in tropical and subtropical waters throughout the world.

66

Although rough-toothed dolphins seldom bowride, when they do it is with great vigor and enthusiasm. (Marc Webber)

For an animal that is relatively playful at sea—leaping, splashing, and frolicking much of the time—this species does not always ride the bow waves of vessels. On occasion, a group of these dolphins will briefly take up station on a bow wave, but they usually seem to lose interest within a few hundred yards and go on their way. Perhaps because of the way they disperse in numerous small groups, they may have a rather small radius of activity, beyond which they encroach on another group's territory. Or maybe they are simply not interested in humans.

On the other hand, rough-toothed dolphins are simply beguiling in captivity. Animal trainers who have dealt with this species often begin to feel like it is they who are being trained, little by little, to do things that the dolphins want to do. Of course, anyone who has had a pet knows that it will often exert its will at training time; but usually a pet will simply be stubborn or modify your game to suit itself. Rough-toothed dolphins often throw in an entirely new game which they expect humans to learn, and they have infinite patience to teach it. Usually that involves getting the trainer wet or humiliated in some way that seems to give great delight to the dolphins.

Virtually nothing is known about the reproductive habits of rough-toothed dolphins. The youngest mature animals reported from a study of 39 individuals from Japan were probably 14 years old for males and 17 for females. By this age, the animals were about 8 feet in length, and the weight ranged from 200 to 320 pounds, with males being more robust. If layers in the teeth accurately reflect age (see the chapter on sperm whales for explanation), the maximum age in this sample of animals was 44 years. Gestation, maximum weight and length, pregnancy rate, and reproductive life span have not been determined. It is of great scientific and curatorial interest, however, that a female of this species mated with a male bottlenose dolphin in captivity at Sea Life Park on Oahu, and produced a healthy hybrid which survived more than ten years. Prior to that, some researchers supposed that rough-toothed dolphins and bottlenose dolphins belonged to entirely different families of cetaceans—as far apart genetically, for example, as wolves and bears. The hybrid died at too young an age to determine its fertility.

Rough-toothed dolphins can be identified at sea by the smooth forehead and dark body with white along the lips and underside. (Robert L. Pitman)

Rough-toothed dolphins (Robert L. Pitman)

STRIPED DOLPHIN
Stenella coeruleoalba

Striped dolphins are deep-ocean creatures, very gregarious with their own kind but usually shy of vessels and other species of marine mammals. In the eastern tropical Pacific "tuna-porpoise" fishery, at least one herd of these fast-swimming dolphins earned the nickname "untouchables" because of their adroit avoidance of the fishing boats. They would virtually disappear over the horizon at the first approach of a vessel, and whatever tuna were associated with them disappeared as well. There is no such "tuna-porpoise" fishery around Hawaii, but it is nonetheless characteristic of the species to flee any approaching vessel. Rarely can they be approached closely enough to be identified; but there are a few records of striped dolphins in the channels between the main Hawaiian Islands, and there is one documented stranding.

Striped dolphins keep to deep water as a rule, and they feed primarily on lantern fish but will also eat squid and shrimp. They travel in large herds numbering from a few hundred to several thousand animals, creating the appearance of shoal water with their splashing leaps. Most of their feeding takes place at night, when their prey species come closer to the surface; during the day, they aggregate and travel in herds. Observation of their normal behavior is made difficult by their quick flight response and nocturnal feeding habits.

It is known from dolphin drive fisheries in Japan, where these animals are caught in large numbers, that females attain sexual maturity at nine years of age and bear a calf about once every four years of their reproductive life, to around age 48. The maximum lifespan noted for females was 57.5 years, but the usual lifespan is more like 50 years. Males also become sexually mature at about nine years of age, but it is possible that full sexual capability is not

Named for the cerulean blue streaks that so dominate their color pattern, striped dolphins are considered one of the most beautiful of all dolphin species. (Marc Webber)

attained until about age 15. Their lifespan seems slightly shorter than that of females, usually a little more than 40 years.

These animals can be readily identified by the well-defined narrow black stripe which runs from the eye to the bottom rear, with another branch from the eye to the leading edge of the flipper. These stripes stand out prominently against the light grey and white colors of the flanks and belly. The color on top is dark bluish grey, creating a strikingly beautiful pattern from which another common name, ''blue and white dolphin'', is derived. Another common name, ''euphrosyne dolphin'', derives from the Greek for ''mirth'', probably from attributing their excited departures to joyous habit.

Striped dolphins travel in large herds and usually stay away from vessels. Quite often, these animals jump high out of the water as they travel rapidly on the ocean's surface. (Robert L. Pitman)

HAWAIIAN SPINNER DOLPHIN
Stenella longirostris

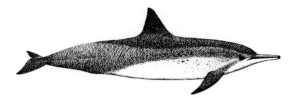

Hawaiian spinner dolphins are a local subspecies of the spinner dolphins or "spinner porpoises" (fishermen's terminology) which are found in tropical oceans throughout the world. The common name derives from their peculiar and spectacular habit of leaping high into the air, spinning like a top many times before falling into the water on their side or back with a resounding slap. The spins may be done repeatedly, sometimes with variations such as cartwheeling, or they may be partial leaps culminating with a vigorous slapping of the body against the water. Many members of a herd may simultaneously and repeatedly spin and frolic in this fashion, giving the appearance that the ocean surface is erupting with dolphins. It is one of the most joyous sights at sea, evoking the feeling that it is done solely for fun; but it may serve as a signal that feeding time is about to begin. It is significant that spinning activity peaks in the midafternoon, before the group spreads out at dusk to forage.

Hawaiian spinner dolphins are distinguished from most other forms of Pacific spinner dolphins by their "three-tone" pigmentation pattern, with a sharply defined dark grey dorsal "cape", a lighter grey side stripe, and a white belly (which appears pink when the blood vessels underlying the blubber are filled, giving rise to an earlier species name of *rosiventris*, meaning rose-colored belly). The snout is long and slender, designed for grasping the relatively small (fist-size), soft-skinned fishes upon which the animals feed during the evening hours. The overall size is 5.5 to 6.5 feet in length and 130 to 200 pounds in weight.

In Hawaiian waters, spinner dolphins gather in large herds at night, offshore and in deep channels between the islands, for feeding; they disperse during the day into smaller groups near shore

The three-toned color pattern of Hawaiian spinner dolphins is clearly evident in this photo taken off the Kona Coast. Spinners are probably the most frequently observed marine mammal in Hawaiian waters throughout the year. (James D. Watt)

and in bays for resting and playing. One of the most famous bays they visit is Kealake'akua Bay on the southern shore of the big island, Hawaii. There they may be found most mornings in a closely knit, resting group of about thirty individuals. Other bays and bights along the Kona coast and other islands also harbor groups of these dolphins, with much interchange between groups. The social structure is not known, but it seems that it may be more fluid and open than is the case for many other toothed whales, which tend to align in kinship groups. Contact is an essential ingredient of the associations in spinner dolphin society, where touching, nuzzling, and stroking occur frequently among all animals in the group, even as group composition changes.

Spinner dolphins become sexually mature at about five years of age, when both males and females are about 5.5 feet in length. Thereafter, the mating is promiscuous, with peak activity during the summer and fall. Gestation takes 10.5 months, and the new-

Spinner dolphins are long, sleek, and graceful animals which like to ride the bow waves of passing ships. In Hawaii, they are extremely shy of divers and seldom allow themselves to be photographed underwater. (Randall S. Wells)

born are about 30 inches in length and weigh only about 33 pounds. Weaning normally occurs within a year, after which time the juvenile dolphins may form subgroups and aggregations with other juveniles for at least part of the time. Even prior to weaning, juveniles may spend increasing amounts of time with other dolphins than their mother. The calving interval is normally about three years, and the maximum lifespan is unknown, but it is probably more than twenty years. Determining age is possible using growth rings in the teeth, but after about 13 years no further laminations are laid down, making maximum age determination problematic.

SPOTTED DOLPHIN
Stenella attenuata

Several species of spotted dolphins inhabit tropical oceans and seas worldwide, and there are many regional varieties as well. Spotted dolphins seen around Hawaii are of the species *S. attenuata,* and often lack the heavy spotting that characterizes sub-species and races in other regions. This causes these slender little dolphins to look superficially similar to spinner dolphins, rough-toothed dolphins, and even bottlenose dolphins, though they are slighter of build than the latter two. They could also be confused at a distance with striped dolphins or Fraser's dolphins, but are generally more willing to ride a bow wave than those oceanic nomads. In order to be sure of identification, one must look for the long, slender, well-demarcated snout with a leading white tip.

Spotted dolphins attain a size of 6.5 to 7 feet and 240 pounds, with males larger than females by about 6 inches and 40 pounds at maturity. The coloration is dark grey on the back and light grey below, with a very dark "cape" from the forehead to the dorsal fin. If spotting is present, it will consist of light spots in the dark field areas, and dark spots in the light. Older individuals are typically much more spotted than juveniles.

These little dolphins are very gregarious and form herds of a few dozen to over a thousand. They are not particularly wary of boats, except in the eastern tropical Pacific, where tuna/dolphin fishing has had a heavy impact (fishing for yellowfin tuna in this area utilizes spinner, spotted, and common dolphins as locators of tuna, and since 1971, over six million dolphins have been killed by entrapment in mile-long tuna nets). Even there, occasionally, they will ride a vessel's bow wave. Around Hawaii, spotted dolphins are fairly common in the passages between islands and far offshore. It is known from tagging studies elsewhere that they travel 30 to 50

Spotted dolphins (Christopher Newbert)

miles a day, and their foraging range is on the order of 200 to 300 miles; those around Hawaii, therefore, may travel around much of the archipelago. They apparently feed on squid and fish in deep water offshore.

Sexual maturity occurs at 11 to 12 years of age for males, when they are about 6.6 feet long. Gestation lasts about 11 months, length at birth is 3 feet, and calves are weaned by about 20 months of age, though some solid food may be taken as early as 6 months. The calving interval varies from about 2.5 to 4 years, and a female may produce half a dozen or more calves in her lifetime. The adult sex ratio in herds is about one male to 1.3 females. The natural life span can exceed 40 years for females and a little less for males. (This accounts for the difference in sex ratio.) Off Japan, where these dolphins have been extensively studied, there are three peaks in mating season: February and March, July, and November.

Hawaiian spotted dolphins often rocket out of the water in spectacular leaps, repeating them over and over again. (Edward Shallenberger)

80

Normally shy of divers, these Hawaiian spotted dolphins approached to investigate light reflected off the photographer's underwater camera. (James D. Watt)

Hawaiian monk seal (Jacki Kilbride)

HAWAIIAN MONK SEAL
Monachus schauinslandi

The most Hawaiian of Hawaii's marine mammals are the monk seals, which are found from Nihoa Island to Kure Island in the leeward Hawaiian Archipelago and range out to sea hundreds of miles from these favorite spots. They are rarely seen around the inhabited main islands of Hawaii, perhaps because they are shy of people historically and they were almost invariably killed whenever encountered. Monk seals are the most ancient and primitive of all living seals: the Hawaiian species and with its two sibling species in the Mediterranean and Caribbean (*M. monachus* and *M. tropicalis*, respectively), remain distinct in the world's tropical and temperate seas while their erstwhile relatives have diverged and diversified toward the earth's colder polar regions. This was an evolutionary mistake, in some respects: not only are the tropical habitats limited in haulout areas and resources, but they subsequently became favored habitats for humans, who are often inclined to kill edible animals and generally rearrange natural areas for human habitation.

The story of the Hawaiian monk seal is tragic indeed. As human activity increased within their habitat, many monk seals were clubbed to death for meat, oil, and skin. Being naturally sensitive to human activities, disturbance on their hauling-out grounds forced mothers and young into the water, where shark predation further reduced the populations. More recently, fishing nets lost by fishermen throughout the North Pacific ultimately drift into the monk seals' habitat, drowning others accidentally.

Today, although totally protected, they remain one of the most endangered of all seals.

Monk seals feed on eels, small reef fish, octopus, and lobsters. They are known to dive to at least 500 feet and remain underwater

In spite of extensive observation in the wild, researchers have yet to witness the birth of a Hawaiian monk seal pup, and so it is thought that they are born at night. (Stanley M. Minasian)

for as long as twenty minutes while foraging. Presumably, they can eat deep-water species as well during their long forays at sea. They may eat as much as 10 percent of their body weight each day, putting on a thick blubber layer as an energy reserve. A pregnant 7-foot-long female, for example, may weigh as much as 600 pounds and lose about half of that during a 35- to 40-day nursing period before her single pup is weaned. The 40-inch-long pup, on the other hand, weighs about 35 to 40 pounds at birth and will quadruple its weight (to 140 pounds) during that nursing period. Then the pup is on its own, losing weight as it slowly learns by trial and error how to feed in the shallow waters around its island of birth. By the time it is a year old, it has typically slimmed down to 100 pounds and grown to 4.5 feet in length. It takes several more years to reach adulthood, when both sexes are about 7 feet in length and weigh between 350 and 400 pounds. The lifespan may extend to 30 years, and most seals remain at their island of birth.

Monk seals are normally polygynous—that is, one male may fertilize many females. At certain islands this has become a bit of a problem, as adult males now outnumber adult females by as much as three to one and they are somewhat aggressive in their courtship. On these islands, females and juveniles have been observed to be severely bitten during the advances of males, and some deaths have

Underwater, Hawaiian monk seals are graceful, fluid, and curious. These animals spend weeks at sea feeding before returning to the islands where they live to sleep and digest their food. (Jacki Kilbride)

occurred as a result. Within recent years, wildlife managers and biologists have taken steps to identify the more aggressive males and move them to outlying areas. In addition, they collect pups which have been separated from their mothers and are often emaciated. These pups are rehabilitated until self-sufficient, and the females are returned to the wild while the males may be kept for eventual placement in marine parks.

The breeding season is during spring and summer. Gestation is estimated to last one year, with most of the births occuring from March to May. The newborn pups have black, fuzzy short hair. During the nursing period, the black hairs molt (fall out) individually and are replaced by silver-grey fur on the back and creamy white fur on the underside, so that by the time weaning occurs the pups look like overgrown silver-grey footballs with large black eyes and whiskers at one end and floppy flippers at the other. Subsequent molts occur annually, with the entire epidermis being shed in ragtag fashion like a snake's skin, revealing a shiny new coat underneath. All 32 of the permanent teeth have erupted by six weeks of

Unlike most other species of pinnipeds, Hawaiian monk seals prefer to rest apart from others of their own kind. (Stanley M. Minasian)

age, but young monk seals are reluctant to use them in defense. Rather, they investigate things playfully with their mouths.*

Taxonomically, Hawaiian monk seals are classified among the pinniped (fin-footed) carnivores, in the family Phocidae (true seals) and subfamily Monachinae (derived from the Greek for "monk", or solitary individual). The genus *Monachus* was described for the Mediterranean monk seal by Hermann in 1779, and the species *M. schauinslandi* was described by Matschie in 1905 after it had nearly been exterminated by commercial sealing in the 1800s. Hawaiian monk seals were rarely seen in the beginning of this century, but 1,206 were counted in the late 1950s during a comprehensive aerial, vessel, and shore survey of all the Hawaiian leeward islands. Similar surveys in the late 1970s produced counts of about half that

---

* One young monk seal on Midway Island, whose progress was followed by the author for its first year, when first weaned would playfully tug at the frayed end of a line hanging from a small boat. By the time it was eight months old, this seal could still be approached when it hauled out, and the tag number on its flipper could be read. Afterward, it rarely came ashore.

many, with most of the decline occuring on the westernmost islands.

Concurrent with the latter census, many sick and dying monk seals came ashore with symptoms of ciguatera poisoning. (Liver samples from two that had died tested positive for the ciguatoxin, as did eels that were prey species in the area.) Ciguatera is a poison that originates in microscopic plankton, and it concentrates mostly in the fatty organs of fish higher in the food chain. It can lead to congestive heart and lung failure in mammals (including humans) that eat the contaminated fish. Aside from poisoning, some seals evidenced significant scarring from shark bites, from which it is assumed that predation from sharks may be an important cause of natural mortality. Some seals showed evidence of entanglement in fishing gear.

Hawaiian monk seals are considered endangered—it is illegal to kill, capture, or harass them, and their habitat should be protected from all human disturbances, including the use of fishing gear which proves to be dangerous to them. The Waikiki Aquarium has maintained monk seals in captivity at various times since 1951 and is now quite successful at it—one seal lived 13 years there.

Except for mothers and their pups, and adult male-female pairs during breeding season, monk seals do not usually haul out together like most other seals. There may be several seals on a beach separated by short distances, but they behave and react as individuals rather than as a group.

The following animals have never been observed in Hawaiian waters and the chances of seeing them in the archipelago are at best remote. However, because of their known range, their occasional presence cannot be totally discounted.

Blue whale flukes (Michael Manolson)

BLUE WHALE
Balaenoptera musculus

Blue whales are the largest animals ever to inhabit the earth. Some have grown larger than 100 feet in length and 180 tons in weight. Their awesome size may have been an advantage for millions of years of evolution, but it became a disadvantage at the beginning of this century, when modern whaling commenced in earnest. Blue whales were among the first whales in the modern era to be slaughtered nearly to extinction for their oil. Populations worldwide were reduced to very small remnants of their original size and most have shown little sign of recovery. Fortunately, the North Pacific stock of blue whales was not reduced as severely as some, and it is possible that these leviathans might visit Hawaiian waters on rare occasions. Most of the North Pacific blue whales winter off Mexico and Central America, where as many as 600 may yet survive.

Blue whales often raise their 15-foot-wide flukes high into the air prior to their lengthy dives. (Michael Manolson)

For the blue whale to survive as a species, international protection must continue and sights like this adult with calf must become more commonplace. (Marine Mammal Fund photograph)

GINKGO-TOOTHED BEAKED WHALE
Mesoplodon ginkgodens

Named for the shape of their two teeth, which resembles the leaf of the ginkgo tree (as well as the spade on playing cards), ginkgo-toothed beaked whales are recently discovered members of the family Ziphiidae. This species was originally described from a 16.5-foot, 3,300-pound specimen that stranded alive at Oiso Beach on Japan's Sagami Bay in 1957; these unusual little whales have since been seen or stranded off California, Mexico, Taiwan, Indonesia, and Sri Lanka. They seem to prefer warm temperate and tropical waters, so they may appear near Hawaii, although thus far none has been sighted. Adults are dark or grey over the whole body, with whitish spots and parallel scars from tooth scratches. They eat squid and generally prefer deep water.

Like many of the beaked whales, ginkgo-toothed beaked whales are seldom seen or confirmed at sea. (Painting by Larry Foster)

FRASER'S DOLPHIN
Lagenodelphis hosei

F raser's dolphins were first described as a separate species by Dr. F.C. Fraser in 1956. The identification was based on a skeleton found on a beach in Sarawak, Borneo, in 1895. Still nothing was known of the external appearance of these little short-snouted dolphins until 1966, when the author photographed a herd in the mid Pacific, near the equator. Finally, in 1972 several more specimens were collected from various parts of the world, and the species could be more fully described at last.

Fraser's dolphins are very shy of vessels, and they look and act like striped dolphins in many ways, except that they have a very short snout and tiny dorsal fin, flippers and flukes. Because they inhabit tropical oceans, they may occasionally visit Hawaiian waters.

The bluish grey and white color pattern of Fraser's dolphins is beautiful and extremely complex. (painting by Larry Foster)

94

Fraser's dolphins are rarely sighted, but when they are, they are usually in large herds of a thousand or more animals. (Robert L. Pitman)

SOUTHERN BOTTLENOSED WHALE
Hyperoodon planifrons

On the same day in 1966 that the author sighted the Fraser's dolphins, he also saw and photographed an interesting herd of beaked whales on the equator near the International Date Line. Nobody could identify these whales either, but in the years since it has become clear that they were southern bottlenosed whales. The distribution of beaked whales in general is not well known, and southern bottlenosed whales in particular were thought to inhabit only the higher latitudes of the southern oceans (whence their name). Several independent documentations have shown otherwise, though: a Dutch captain, W.F.J. Morzer-Bruyns, had seen them near the Galapagos Islands a few years before this author's sighting, and more recently, Japanese researchers have seen and photographed them off Okinawa. Since they occur that far north into the North Pacific, they cannot be discounted as possible visitors to Hawaiian waters.

Southern bottlenosed whales grow to a length of 20 to 30 feet. They look and act like Baird's beaked whales, but the forehead is more bulging, the rostrum more slender, and the dorsal fin significantly larger. The coloration is acorn brown overall, lighter on the forehead and with a dark band around the head just behind the blowhole. They are gregarious creatures and sometimes approach vessels.

Southern bottlenosed whales are very gregarious animals, forming herds of up to several dozen individuals. (painting by Larry Foster)

This group of southern bottlenosed whales was filmed by the author in the mid Pacific Ocean near the International Date Line in 1966. (Kenneth C. Balcomb III)

SUGGESTED READING

Baker, Alan. *Whales and Dolphins from New Zealand and Australia.* Wellington, Australia: Victoria University Press, 1983.

Ellis, Richard. *The Book of Dolphins.* New York: Alfred A. Knopf, 1983.

Ellis, Richard. *The Book of Whales.* New York: Alfred A. Knopf, 1980.

Haley, Delphine, ed. *Marine Mammals of the North Pacific and Arctic Waters.* Revised edition. Seattle: Pacific Search Press, 1986.

Hoyt, Erich. *The Whale Watcher's Handbook.* Toronto, Canada: Madison Press, Ltd., 1984.

Kaufmann, Gregory D. and Forestell, Paul H. *Hawaii's Humpback Whales.* Kihei, Hawaii: Pacific Whale Foundation, 1986.

Leatherwood, Stephen and Reeves, Randall R. *The Sierra Club Handbook of Whales and Dolphins.* San Francisco: Sierra Club Books, 1983.

Leatherwood, Stephen; Reeves, Randall R.; Perrin, William F., and Evans, William E. *The Whales, Dolphins, and Porpoises of the Eastern North Pacific and Adjacent Arctic Waters.* Revised edition. US Commerce Department, NOAA, Technical Report NMFS Circular 444, 1982.

McIntyre, Joan. *Mind in the Waters.* New York: Charles Scribner's Sons, 1974.

Minasian, Stanley M.; Balcomb, Kenneth C., and Foster, Larry. *The World's Whales.* Washington DC: Smithsonian Books, 1984.

Nishiwaki, Masaharu. *Whales and Pinnipeds.* Tokyo, Japan: University of Tokyo Press, 1965.

Norris, Kenneth S. *The Porpoise Watcher.* New York: W.W. Norton, 1974.

Scheffer, Victor B. *The Natural History of Marine Mammals.* New York: Charles Scribner's Sons, 1976.

Shallenberger, Edward W. *The Status of Hawaiian Cetaceans.* Springfield, Virginia: National Technical Information Service, US Department of Commerce, 1981.

ORDER FORM

The Whales of Hawaii is a unique publication and a perfect gift for friends traveling to Hawaii.

"Watching the Whales" is a half-hour video production presenting nine species of whales and dolphins. Displayed with incredible surface and underwater sequences, common, spinner, spotted, and whitebeak dolphins, as well as pilot whales, killer whales, gray whales, humpback whales, and blue whales are presented without narration or music, just their natural surface and underwater sounds.

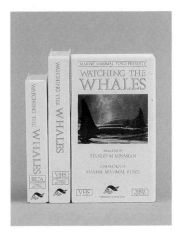

☐ Please send_____copy(ies) of *The Whales of Hawaii* at $9.95 per copy;

☐ Please send_____copy(ies) of "Watching the Whales" video tape at $39.95 per copy, _____VHS_____BETAMAX;

All items will be sent third-class mail. Please include $1.50 per item for shipping and handling. California residents add 6½% sales tax.

☐ I have enclosed a check or money order totaling $_____.

☐ I wish to charge my MC/VISA #_____,

expiring_____. Signature_____.

Name_____

Address_____

City_____State_____Zip_____

Mail to: Marine Mammal Fund,
Fort Mason Center, Building E, San Francisco, CA 94123.